The Law Behind Your Real Estate Portfolio

Understanding Real Estate Laws to Safeguard Your Investment

JEFFREY S LOOMIS

The Law Behind Your Real Estate Portfolio

Copyright

Copyright © by Jeffrey S. Loomis 2024. All rights reserved.

Before this document is duplicated or reproduced in any manner, the publisher's consent must be gained. Therefore, the contents within can neither be stored electronically, transferred, nor kept in a database. Neither in Part nor full can the document be copied, scanned, faxed, or retained without approval from the publisher or creator.

The Law Behind Your Real Estate Portfolio

Table Of Contents

Copyright..1
Table Of Contents...2
Dedication...5
About the Author..6
Introduction..10
Chapter 1..15
Introduction To Real Estate Laws.......................15
Property Law..31
Terminologies And Concepts In Real Estate Law... 40
Chapter Two...69
Real Estate Ownership Types.............................69
What is meant by "Property Ownership?.............69
Steps to Take In Due Diligence Before Purchasing Real Estate..85
Chapter Three...106
Recognizing Important Terms, Types, And Avoidable Pitfalls in Real Estate Contracts......................106
Real Estate Contract Types..............................108
Important Words and Clauses to Search For.........111
Typical Errors to Steer Clear Of......................115
Strategies for Bargaining with Tenants on Lease Terms...118
How to Write Terms of Lease That Are Fair to Both Parties...124
Strategies For Bargaining With Tenants On Lease

Terms.. 132
It's vital to be ready to handle any questions, concerns, or negotiations a tenant may have regarding the lease you issued. You don't want to reject adjustments or shut them off immediately. Rather, engage the topic with an open mind. These are some ideas for deciding on lease terms with tenants... 132
OWNERSHIP OF PROPERTY................................. 136
Externalities of Property Rights............................ 142
Characteristics of Property Rights........................ 153
Chapter 4... 158
What Does Joint Tenancy Mean When Owning Property?... 158
THE OPERATION OF JOINT TENANCY................... 160
Establishing Joint Tenancy.................................... 164
The Financial Effects of Co-Tenancy...................... 172
Breaking Up a Joint Tenancy................................. 174
Benefits and Drawbacks of Co-Tenancy................ 176
Drawbacks of Co-Tenancy..................................... 180
Chapter Five... 190
Zoning Laws... 190
An Overview Of How They Affect Property Development.. 190
Zoning's Effect on Real Estate Development......... 192
Environmental Law and Transactions in Real Estate.. 197
Handling Environmental Difficulties in Real Estate Deals.. 202
Important Steps to Finish the Title Search Procedure

205

Crucial Phases in the Title Search Procedure....... 208
Chapter Six..218
Techniques For Asset Protection............................218
Asset Protection.. 222
What Is It?...222
Techniques for the Protection of Assets.................225
In summary...232
Advice for Safeguarding Assets............................ 234
How to resolve disputes concerning borders........236
Solutions for the Situation......................................238
What Constitutes a Real Estate Contract Breach?244
Navigating Changing Legal Regulations in Real Estate... 247
Market News Real Estate Investments................... 247
Techniques for Handling Changing Legal Requirements...253

Dedication

To my family, whose unwavering support and encouragement have made this journey possible. To my mentors and colleagues, whose wisdom and guidance have shaped my understanding of real estate law. And to the countless investors and professionals who strive to navigate the complexities of the real estate world with integrity and insight. **This book is for you.**

JEFFERY S LOOMIS

About the Author

Jeffrey S Loomis is a renowned real estate writer who has established himself as a trusted authority in the industry. With a passion for real estate and a deep understanding of the legal frameworks involved, Loomis has dedicated his career to educating and empowering individuals in their real estate endeavors.

Drawing from his extensive experience and expertise, Loomis has authored several influential books, including "Mastering Virtual Real Estate Wholesaling: Unveiling the Online Blueprint for Success with Minimal Tools," "Virtual Real Estate Gold: Unveiling the Wholesaling Secret in the Digital Age," and "Real Estate Financing: Strategies for Structuring Debt and Equity." These publications have garnered widespread acclaim for their practical insights and actionable advice, making Loomis a sought-after resource for aspiring real estate professionals, seasoned investors, and anyone seeking to navigate the complex landscape of real estate law.

In "The Law Behind Your Real Estate Portfolio," Loomis leverages his profound knowledge of real estate laws to provide readers with a comprehensive guide to safeguarding their investments. From the fundamentals of real estate law to the nuances of different ownership structures, Loomis covers essential topics that are crucial for anyone involved in real estate transactions. With a keen eye for detail and a knack for simplifying complex legal concepts, Loomis equips readers with the tools and knowledge necessary to make informed decisions and protect their assets.

Through his writing, Loomis demonstrates a commitment to empowering individuals in their real estate journeys. His ability to break down complex legal principles into digestible and practical advice sets him apart as a trusted authority in the field. Whether you are a novice investor or a seasoned professional, **"The Law Behind Your Real Estate Portfolio"** serves as an indispensable resource tool, guiding you through the difficult web of real estate laws and ensuring that your investments are safeguarded.

Introduction

Welcome to "The Law Behind Your Real Estate Portfolio: Understanding Real Estate Laws to Safeguard Your Investment." Whether you're a seasoned investor or just beginning your journey in the dynamic world of real estate, this book is your comprehensive guide to navigating the complex legal landscape that underpins every successful property venture.

I'm Jeffrey S. Loomis, and for over two decades, I've immersed myself in the intricacies of real estate, not just as a writer but as a passionate advocate for informed and strategic investment. The real estate market, with its promise of wealth and security, is equally fraught with legal challenges and pitfalls that can turn lucrative opportunities into costly misadventures. This book aims to arm you with the knowledge necessary to steer clear of those pitfalls and make informed decisions that will safeguard your investments for years to come.

In these pages, you will find clear and practical explanations of the essential aspects of real estate law. We'll start with the fundamentals, offering a thorough introduction to real estate laws that govern your transactions and property management. From understanding the different types of real estate ownership—whether it's fee simple, leasehold, or joint tenancy—to recognizing the crucial terms embedded in real estate contracts, you'll gain the insights needed to navigate and negotiate with confidence.

One of the critical areas we will explore is the significance of joint tenancy in property ownership. Understanding the legal implications of how you hold title to your property can have profound effects on your estate planning and asset protection strategies. We'll also delve into zoning laws, often an overlooked aspect of real estate investment, but one that can dramatically impact your property's value and development potential.

In addition to these core topics, this book will guide you through the maze of asset protection

The Law Behind Your Real Estate Portfolio

techniques, helping you develop robust strategies to shield your investments from unforeseen legal and financial threats. You'll learn how to create a fortress around your portfolio, ensuring that your hard-earned assets remain secure against **lawsuits, creditors, and economic downturns.**

My goal with "The Law Behind Your Real Estate Portfolio" is not just to educate, but to empower you. By understanding the legal framework that governs real estate, you'll be better equipped to make decisions that are not only profitable but also legally sound. You'll gain the confidence to tackle complex transactions, negotiate favorable terms, and ultimately build a portfolio that stands the test of time.

Let's embark on this journey together and unlock the full potential of your real estate investments with a solid foundation in the law.

Jeffrey S. Loomis

Chapter 1

Introduction To Real Estate Laws

Laws about real estate control the myriad of aspects that are involved in the process of buying, keeping, and selling real estate. The field of law is always growing, as new developments in technology and economic conditions are absorbed into the laws that are already in place. A grasp of real estate law is essential to successfully manage the legal issues that it presents and to realize the benefits that it delivers. In this chapter, we will investigate the multiple aspects of real estate law, including its guiding acts, the rights and obligations that it bestows, and how its provisions are implemented in a variety of situations.

The relationship that exists between a landlord and a tenant is one of the most important aspects of real estate, and this is true for both residential and commercial structures. The existence of this link is strongly connected to the definitions of property ownership and renting, which have been established by the law. There are numerous parallels between residential and commercial landlord and tenant agreements; yet, there are also substantial differences between the two. In this essay, we will address these contrasts, with a particular focus on the legal features of conventional residential and commercial leases, as well as the rights and responsibilities of both the landlord and the tenant.

When it comes to being a landlord, having ownership of both residential and commercial real estate comes with several benefits as well as challenges. Landlording is a solid source of cash that may be utilized to cover obligations like mortgages and other costs, states Jeffrey. This is particularly advantageous in the commercial real estate market, as rental money may be utilized to pay for maintenance and operating needs.

Furthermore, having tenants for a lengthy term develops a sense of stability and security, which is another advantage of being a landlord.

However, owning a home has its own set of issues. For instance, a landlord has complete responsibility for the expensive and time-consuming care and repairs of the property. In addition, a landlord needs to make sure that their property conforms with all legal standards and be educated about all relevant laws and regulations in their neighborhood. Lastly, managing renters may be tough since landlords need to make sure that all rental agreement responsibilities are completed and that tenants are aware of their rights.

In conclusion, owning a piece of residential or commercial real estate may be a gratifying experience for a landlord. To be ready for the duties that come with this job, it is necessary to grasp the benefits and problems that come with it.

The topic of real estate law is complicated and dynamic. It deals with the control of property ownership, including rules regulating ownership transfers, tenant rights, and landlord responsibilities. State and federal legislation,

The Law Behind Your Real Estate Portfolio

case law, and administrative regulations are the key sources of real estate law.

Real estate law also encompasses various other issues, such as zoning rules, property law, contract law, and land use law. Anyone participating in the buying, sale, or leasing of real estate must have a basic grasp of real estate law.

Real estate contracts are controlled by contract law, which also stipulates the terms of the agreement and the penalties for noncompliance. Property law includes trespassing remedies as well as ownership and use rights of real properties. Local and state zoning regulations, as well as zoning standards, determine how land is utilized. In general, zoning laws outline the sorts of activities that are authorized on a given piece of land.

Lastly, both buyers and sellers must know the tax repercussions of real estate transactions. A real estate transaction may have considerable tax repercussions, so it's vital to contact an experienced tax professional to make sure all appropriate taxes are paid.

In conclusion, anybody involved in real estate transactions must have a basic knowledge of real estate law because it is a sophisticated issue. It's vital to know the roots of real estate law, its

The Law Behind Your Real Estate Portfolio

numerous subfields, and how real estate transactions affect taxes. Landlords, buyers, and sellers should all make sure that all taxes are paid and that their rights are respected by possessing the essential information.

When making decisions affecting their property, homeowners should consider real estate laws. Zoning regulations, property taxes, mortgages, and other concerns surrounding the ownership, use, and transfer of real estate are all handled under this field of law. It also addresses the obligations and rights that come with being a homeowner, such as the right to privacy, the capacity to sue for injury or damage the property causes, and the responsibility to protect the property. It's vital to talk with a qualified real estate lawyer if you want to understand more about the laws. Homeowners may acquire extensive legal advice on the proper course of action as well as aid in understanding their legal rights and duties from an attorney. They may also advise how to handle disagreements originating from ownership or use of real estate, as well as how to stay clear of any legal complications. Homeowners may defend their rights and interests and make knowledgeable decisions regarding their property by being aware of the foundations of real estate law.

The Law Behind Your Real Estate Portfolio

A large variety of legal matters are handled in the complicated field of real estate law. To preserve their rights and interests, citizens must be informed of the basis of real estate law. This covers key principles like contracts, mortgages, zoning, development, and property ownership. Laws regulating the transfer of ownership of land, buildings, and other real estate are covered under **property ownership**. The use of land is controlled by **zoning and development restrictions,** which also describe what may be placed there. Mortgages are used to finance the purchase of real estate, whereas contracts are used to acquire

The Law Behind Your Real Estate Portfolio

or lease property. Numerous state and federal rules control each of these areas. To preserve their rights and interests, citizens must be informed of the basis of real estate law. People may make sure that their rights and interests are preserved when participating in real estate transactions by being knowledgeable of the principles of the law. Furthermore, having a basic knowledge of real estate law may aid individuals in making sensible decisions concerning the purchasing and selling of real estate.

The Law Behind Your Real Estate Portfolio

Real estate law is a complex topic of law that deals with many various elements of purchasing, selling, and utilizing real estate. It handles intricate regulations involving contracts, taxes, repossession, title disputes, and leasing, among other things. Those who are buying, selling, or simply attempting to protect themselves from **exploitation** may find it beneficial to learn the principles of real estate law because they give exact standards and laws for the landlord's behavior about rent, maintenance, and other concerns. In addition, these regulations offer landlords the ability to dismiss tenants who don't fulfill the requirements of the lease, enabling the enforcement of the rules controlling the real estate market. All things considered, landlord-tenant rules are an important weapon for governing the real estate business and guaranteeing the rights of both landlords and tenants.

To sum up, real estate laws are vital to know because they affect several transactions including the acquisition and selling of real estate, as well as zoning restrictions, landlord and tenant laws, and the processing of titles to protect both buyers and sellers. A successful transaction for all parties involved may be

The Law Behind Your Real Estate Portfolio

secured by having a basic grasp of real estate law.

Property Law

A subject of law known as property law deals with the acquisition, ownership, use, regulation, and transfer of real and personal property.

The Law Behind Your Real Estate Portfolio

Property law controls numerous parts of how persons use, distribute, and divide their resources, both tangible and immaterial. Property law is a key legal framework that people utilize every day to preserve their rights and the rights of others. It has been around for millennia. The essential notions of property law, the categories of property controlled by it, and the mechanisms for assigning, distributing, and regulating resources will all be explored in this section of this book.

One essential mechanism for protecting real estate rights is property law. This form of regulation is important to build a stable and effective real estate market. Without it, neither buyers or sellers could have faith in the fairness and openness of the transaction process. Throughout the transaction process, both buyers and sellers are protected legally under property law. It ensures that vendors are paid what they expect and that buyers acquire the rights they purchased. Moreover, it empowers parties to govern land ownership and to transfer property ownership. The rights of landowners and how they use their property are also determined by property law. This assures that property owners have the flexibility to employ their property as they see appropriate and can protect their rights against anyone seeking to take advantage of them. The real estate market could not function securely and efficiently without property law. It is therefore a fundamental aspect of safeguarding real estate rights.

Private property rights are secured in great part by property law.

Property law is the branch of law concerned with the rights and obligations of persons about tangible things, such as land, buildings, and personal property, because they enable individuals to own and possess goods that they may use and benefit from, private ownership rights are vital to a healthy society. Property law creates limitations to restrict others from intruding on someone's property and strives to assure that these rights are enforced. These constraints may take the type of monetary prizes, physical restrictions, or even legal punishments for persons who infringe on private property rights. Property law may also be used to conserve the environment, resolve personal issues, and promote economic growth. Property law promotes people's sense of security and stability in their lives by guaranteeing them that their rights to private property will be upheld.

The ownership and use of both real and personal property are controlled by the large and complicated domain of property law. To defend their rights and interests, both persons and companies need to have a basic knowledge of property law. **Real property** and **Personal property** are the two basic forms of property that are recognized under property law. Personal property includes anything that can be moved, such as furniture and automobiles, whereas real property consists of land, fixtures, and buildings. Along with the rights of third parties over property, property law also covers the obligations and rights of property owners. Furthermore, property law deals with problems like zoning rules, condominiums, mortgages, leases, and easements.

Comprehending the foundations of property law may benefit both persons and companies in managing their legal obligations and rights while preserving their property assets.

The objective of property law is to defend the rights of owners of land, buildings, and other forms of property. It is a crucial and difficult subject of law. Property law guarantees that there is as little uncertainty as possible about who owns what elements of a property, helps owners seek reasonable payment for damages to their property, and allows the orderly transfer of property ownership from one person to another. Tenants and anyone who uses other people's property are also covered by property law, which creates criteria for landlord responsibility and tenant rights. Every community requires property law to work, and individuals should be aware of their rights and obligations under the considerable protections this area of the law offers.

Terminologies And Concepts In Real Estate Law

It could be challenging to navigate your way around court papers and processes. To aid you in understanding the process, below are some words you may encounter when buying or selling real estate.

The Contract for Real Estate

The parties agree as follows in consideration for the covenants and agreements mentioned herein as well as for other good and useful recompense, the receipt and sufficiency of which are consequently acknowledged:

1. Entities

Between **Party 1** and **Party 2** (henceforth referred to as the **"Parties"**), this Agreement is entered into on this **[Date]**.

2. Description of the Property

By this agreement, the Parties accept and have accessed the property and knows how the Property looks like and where it's situated.

3. The Acquisition Price and Payment Conditions

For the amount of Purchase Price, Party 1 agrees to acquire the Property, and Party 2 agrees to receive such money as full and final payment for the sale of the Property.

4. Statements and Guarantees

Each Party declares and assures the other that it has all the necessary permission to enter into this Agreement and to carry out all of its duties.

5. Final Words

On [Closing Date], at a venue to be specified by mutual agreement, the transaction will be completed.

6. The Law that Governs

The laws of the state of **[State Name]** shall regulate and interpret this Agreement.

7. Complete Agreement

All prior oral and written agreements, talks, and understandings concerning the subject matter of this agreement are superseded, and this agreement reflects the whole understanding between the Parties.

8. Signatures

Aware Of The Fact That, as of the first indicated date above, the Parties hereto have executed this Agreement.

When discussing real estate titles, the word "clear title" refers to ownership that is valid and undisputed. Liens on the property are one example of a possible matter of conflict.

Finishing

The final step of the contract is the real estate closing. All paperwork, insurance policies, and financing documents are signed and exchanged at the closing. The money that was left over is paid. Depending on the location, a title business, escrow holder, or real estate attorney frequently handles the closing process.

Final Lawyer

The closing lawyer serves a range of functions, and they typically act as the mortgage lender's agent. The closing procedure is monitored by the lawyer, who also makes sure that each party

The Law Behind Your Real Estate Portfolio

understands what they are signing. The closing attorney may give advice and aid in guiding the parties through the decision-making process along the path. Among the tasks include,:

Title Exam

Acquiring title insurance examines documents

★ Money distribution

★ Planning for several gatherings

Common housing is an organization that owns a group of units and the common areas that the inhabitants use. Each tenant owns a piece of the property, which permits them to live in the townhouse or apartment as if they were the original owners.

Act of Faith

Act of Faith is a legal mechanism used in certain countries to guarantee real estate to secure funding. The complete repayment of the agreed-upon loan amount is secured by the assets stated in the deed of trust.

Inaccurate Title

When a property's title is ambiguous or has an encumbrance not mentioned in the deed, or none of these scenarios apply. Judgments and liens are instances of encumbrances.

Easement

The phrase "easement" denotes a party's permission to access or exploit another party's territory for a given purpose. Easements are normally constructed with the best interests of all parties in mind and are expressly meant for nearby properties. They are created by recorded acts. Even if a single individual may be permitted access to the property, the owner nonetheless maintains ownership rights. To acquire access to a common road, sewage (both above and below ground), electricity lines, or if you must pass one property to reach the point of entry, you would need to construct an easement.

Payment

Payment in Full is a payment made in the process of a real estate agreement to reflect the buyer's intention to acquire a property. A purchase and sell agreement is given with the earnest payments. The earnest money is normally kept by the receiver if the agreement is broken.

An Equitable

An Equitable Lien is issued by a court order and is meant to prohibit a property owner from being unfairly benefited. When someone else unjustly acquires a property or makes financial investments in repairs while assuming they are the owner, equitable liens may be employed.

Escrow

An escrow account is where vital money for a real estate sale is held. The account, which is monitored by a third-party escrow service, is kept until all terms and conditions have been completed.

Escrow Agent

The person or entity in charge of handling the money and documentation involved in a real estate transaction. All parties to the transaction are represented by the escrow agents.

Instructions for Escrow

★ 1) All assets and cash controlled by one or more persons

★ 2) A deceased person's possessions are allotted by their will to heirs or beneficiaries.

Estate in Full

A title that is jointly held by a husband and wife. Each individual has an equal right to the full property. By right of survivorship, the surviving spouse is entitled to the title in the case of the death of the other.

Estate Duty

When a deceased person's assets move to their new heirs and beneficiaries, a federal tax is placed on them.

Removal

Removal is the process of driving someone from a property. Likewise known as expulsion. is generally referencing a property tenant.

An exception

The transfer of ownership does not include a notice in the real estate deed of title that defines individual interests or life estates.

Mortgage Repossession when a borrower fails on a mortgage and the mortgage holder sells the property. The profits from the sale are transferred to the lender following the transaction.

Sale of Foreclosure

Sale of Foreclosure is the procedure by which the property is placed up for public auction following the foreclosure. Using the unpaid promissory note as payment, the lender may put a bid on the property. This leads to a cheap purchase.

Horizontal Property Regimes (HPR)

Obtaining ownership of the ground underlying the residence and its contents. Nevertheless, the property that encircles the home and the yard are generally communal spaces and do not belong to the owner. HPRs are typically encountered in condominiums and cooperatives.

Immobile when a property owner is required to traverse another's land even when there is no public entrance or exit on their own. An easement may occasionally be employed to travel over the section of the land that the other party needs to use if this case happens.

Owner of Land

Owner of Land a person or organization that owns real estate and rents it out for profit. Tenant is the word used to denote the person renting the property.

Tenant and Landlord a legal relationship that exists between the renter and the landlord. The rights of the renter and the owner are protected by the law.

Tenant's Lien

A landlord may utilize the money from the sale of personal possessions left by a tenant to settle any outstanding rent or repairs to the property.

Rent a legal contract that provides the renter access to the property for a certain length of time. The conditions of the lease will include the location, late payment fees, and termination methods.

Tenancy-based refers to the space that is covered by the lease. It may also refer to a scenario in which a party develops real estate

and rents it to the building's owner for a prolonged duration.

Lien any legal claim made to collect money or property. The formal papers that the individual who is owing money has signed could also be utilized. If necessary, a lien authorizes the property to be sold. The Lienor is the owner of the lien or the money belongs to the other party.

Lis Pendens

The meaning of this Latin term is **"suit pending."** It's a legal document delivered to parties to alert them that a real estate dispute has been filed. After it is drafted, the defendant is informed by filing it with the County Register of Deeds.

Basis

The land and the buildings/structures on it are referred to as the premises. Premises refers to "all that has hereinabove been stated" in legal terminology.

Calm Title is the technique required to establish who owns a piece of property. An interested party may bring a quiet title action to secure a court order establishing ownership of a property in the case of a dispute regarding who owns it.

Silent Title Action the procedure of commencing a silent title action. The goal of the quiet title lawsuit is to identify who owns the property.

Release and Reclaim Deed

A quitclaim, which is commonly filed between persons who know one other well, such as spouses and family members, transmits an interest in real land without any promises.

Property Agreement

A real estate contract, usually referred to as a purchase agreement, is a written agreement between parties involving the sale of real estate. The obligations of the buyer and seller before title transfer during the closing process are stated in the purchase agreement.

Investment Trust for Real Estate

This investment opportunity, also referred to as a **REIT**, is one in which a business locates investors and acquires real estate. The corporation gives cash to the investor in the form of a secured loan or a share of the property.

Headline

The right to claim ownership of a piece of property and to use it as you see suitable is known as a title. A deed is not the same as a title. The true document indicating who owns the property is the **deed**. Legal rights are referred to as **"titles."**

A Title Agency

A Title Agency is an agent who, on behalf of a title insurance agency, issues or is permitted to issue policies. Also termed an agent for title insurance. In partnership with title insurance firms, title insurance agents undertake property-related research. Any information that could impact the ownership or transfer of the property is obtained via research.

Title Insurance Provider

Title insurance firms frequently referred to as underwriters for title insurance, provide policies for title insurance in exchange for the collection of premiums, part of which are normally remitted to the issuing agent. Title Provisional is a policy of insurance that an insurance company provides. Title insurance is meant to cover the owner, lender, or other interested parties if a title problem surfaces and threatens their interests in the real estate. Legal expenditures and "damages" will be reimbursed.

Title Compiler Title processors engage with parties involved in a real estate transaction to ensure that all documents are submitted appropriately. They aid with preparation, submission, and documentation.

Report Title

A report that offers information about a property's title. Claims, liens, and other troubles against the estate are typically disclosed in the title report. A title report is generated by a title business.

Title Lookup

The method for acquiring records and information on real estate. The chain of title, existing ownership, unpaid property taxes, judgments, and other liens are typical instances of information.

☐ *Underwriter the person or corporation that underwrites a policy of insurance.*

☐ *A Guarantee Certificate is a legal document that provides the property buyer with a legitimate title guarantee.*

Chapter Two

Real Estate Ownership Types

What is meant by "Property Ownership?

Being a property owner includes more than simply purchasing and registering real estate. It encompasses several forms and combinations, each having distinct financial, practical, and legal repercussions. Depending on the ownership structure established, individuals may have varying tax and estate planning duties. These intricacies may have a huge impact on future events, like inheritance or tax assessments; consequently, it's crucial to comprehend them.

Remember that these are only guidelines and that there may be additional solutions available for your situation. Seek guidance from a real estate lawyer to establish your options if you're not sure what sort of property will work best.

1. Exclusive Possession

Owner type: Sole ownership

Sole ownership refers to a scenario in which one individual owns all of the property. They don't need anyone's permission to sell, lease, or otherwise offer the property to someone else, as they are the only proprietors. When a single owner dies away, their property is put into probate until their will is properly accepted.

Advantages:

You are in absolute charge of all decisions concerning the property.

Cons:

Transferring real estate to your heirs at an already stressful and painful moment may be worsened by the long and costly probate process, especially if your heir needs to sell the property because they cannot afford it.

2. Rights of survivorship in Joint Tenancy

Married couples are the sort of owners.

For married couples, joint tenancy with rights of survivorship—which provides each spouse with undivided ownership—is the most frequent sort of property ownership. Each party has equal access rights to the property and equal responsibilities and financial duties for it, including **Maintenance** and **Repair Expenditures.**

One owner in a joint venture may transfer or sell their portion of the property without the other owners' agreement.

Advantages:

Upon the death of one owner, the property promptly passes to the remaining owner without going through probate.

Cons:

A creditor may properly demand a sale to recoup outstanding liabilities from one owner.

A share cannot be given from one heir to another, like a child.

3. Tenants for the total amount

Married couples are the sort of owners.

Instead, married couples may opt to own property as tenants by the entirety, which is identical to Joint Tenancy with the distinction that, as the couple is recognized as a single legal person, an owner cannot do anything with their ownership half without their spouse's agreement. Tenants in common will instantly have their ownership structure amended by a divorce.

Advantages:

The other spouse must be paid for their ownership interest if one spouse is compelled to sell the property to pay off debt.

4. Common land

Married couples are the sort of owners.

There are just 10 community property states in the United States. According to this manner of real estate ownership, even if a property is only registered in one spouse's name, it is nonetheless considered "community property"—that is, property owned by both spouses—if acquired by a spouse during their marriage. This includes every property that was purchased during the marriage.

California, Arizona, Idaho, Nevada, Louisiana, New Mexico, Texas, Washington, and Wisconsin are among the states that accept community property. Residents of Alaska have the opportunity to sign a common property agreement. In California, Nevada, and Washington, registered domestic partnerships are regulated by the same community property regulations.

Advantages:

Equal rights to the property exist between the spouses, and any sale or transfer of the property needs their agreement.

Cons:

Due to this legislation, even if a debt is solely in one spouse's name, any real estate acquired during a marriage may be auctioned by a debt collector to settle the sum.

5. Common Tenancy

Unrelated multiple owners of the same property are one form of owner. Each tenant has a unique deed for how they present the property while they own it as a tenancy in common. For instance, four owners may partition the property into four equal portions, or one owner may own half and the other three, one-sixth each, own the other half.

Since renters do not have survivorship rights, they are free to sell, transfer, or otherwise dispose of their ownership stake without the other owners' approval. Upon the death of a tenant, ownership is transmitted into probate and then to any chosen heirs.

Advantages:

To lower your portion of the mortgage, taxes, and maintenance fees, you may add owners at any point.

Cons:

Without the other tenants' approval, a tenant is allowed to sell or leave their piece of property to whomever they please. The other tenants in common are accountable for making up any gap if one tenant stops paying their part of the rent and taxes.

6. Co-ownership, LLC ownership, partnership ownership

Unrelated multiple owners of the same property are one form of owner.

(LLC), Real estate may be organized as a limited liability corporation (LLC), with ownership shares accessible to numerous owners. Since the owners' money is kept separate from the LLC, this sort of co-ownership for real estate protects them and provides for greater privacy than a tenancy in common. Without the consent of the other shareholders, an owner may sell their LLC ownership at any point. Owners have the choice to employ Pacaso or another independent firm to establish the LLC.

Advantages:

Since an LLC doesn't pay property taxes directly, you may save a lot of money on taxes each year.

Individuals and LLCs give you the possibility to co-own a property with other individuals, such as TIC, but they also provide you with legal protection if something goes wrong on your land.

It's more private than purchasing a home in the old-fashioned manner because only the LLC's name is attached to the property.

Cons:

Contracts and other fees are essential for the establishment and maintenance of an LLC, and they may be exorbitant when done alone.

Steps to Take In Due Diligence Before Purchasing Real Estate

Purchasing a house may be extremely tough, before making any sort of property transaction, one needs to consider numerous concerns and carry out due diligence. Nonetheless, we would encourage any investor intending to acquire real estate to conduct two basic kinds of due diligence operations. These key steps are:

1. Examining physically

Visiting the property is the initial step in the physical inspection procedure, especially if it's a landed property. There are some key elements you should examine and keep an eye out for when you visit the real estate property. The following is covered in a physical condition evaluation of real estate.

a. Pipeline or Power Line: This is a warning indicator that you shouldn't even contemplate purchasing the property further because it is highly unsafe and you could lose it soon if it is placed immediately below or above a power line.

b. Road Alignment: Half or the full property may be directly on the road alignment. This is a poor deal since, should you persist with the purchase, all or a part of the land may end up being worthless owing to confiscation or future public interest.

C. Flooding in the Environment: It's a well-known truth that the rainy season is the optimum time to inspect a property you're contemplating acquiring. When attempting to purchase property in the USA, you have to be wary of regions that are water-locked or prone to floods. Other communities may require their members to employ a boat to get to their homes during the rainy seasons, and other properties may have drainage concerns. These are the things that you should be aware of.

d. Signage: Another key thing to examine is the existence of warning signs like **"buyer beware," "this beware,"** and **"this property is not for sale."** These are property signs—signals that you ought to seek out more about. When you locate these symptoms on a property, it implies that you should make a comprehensive study before opting to pay for it.

e. Verify Occupancy: You must determine whether the property you wish to acquire is inhabited by persons, either via a lease or rental. For example, you may see various landed properties with mini-block industries, mechanic workshops, etc. In most situations, the owner has some form of arrangement with these persons, and they may be the owner's tenants since they don't presently have use of the property and don't want to keep it uninhabited while they hunt for a buyer. When you notice anything like this, you should investigate more about the folks who leased them out and the ones who put them there. By doing so, you will be able to determine the genuine owner of the property.

f. unoccupied: You should validate the vacant state of any property or apartment you wish to acquire. Whether a tenant is presently dwelling in the house, you may want to find out when they will be leaving the property and whether they are prepared to sell it. Example **Quality of Finishing**: You need to be certain about the house's finishing when seeking to acquire a property in USA. Even if you could simply tear out the finishing if you don't like it, it would aid you enormously in the negotiation. Additionally, inspect for wall cracks. Although wall cracks could be crucial, fundamental, or sometimes tiny, they shouldn't be neglected. To establish whether cracks are significant or tiny, however, you should find out why they are there if you discover any in especially fragile regions of the building.

h. Water quality is an extra vital aspect that demands your attention. Make sure to study the water faucet, turn it on, and note the sort of water that emerges. You may want to make sure the developer constructed a functional water treatment system and an appropriate borehole, You should double-check these things before acquiring land in USA, as it would be terrible if the water flowing from your tap is colored or smells weird.

History: This is an important aspect that you should find out by conversing with the residents who live near the property. Even if you don't believe fairy tales exist, you still need to exercise great care and pay close attention to even the tiniest detail regarding the history of any house you choose to acquire. You could ask others who are staying nearby about their knowledge of the property. If you don't get in contact with them, they might opt not to get in touch with you to notify you that there could be a terrible agent out there misleading people with real estate, or possibly he has sold the same real estate to other people. As a consequence, you may query simply, "What do you know about this property? When was it last vacant?" and "Are you familiar with the owner? You can never be too careful, you know, so please exercise extra caution to ensure that you don't wind up in the wrong hands.

But if you're confident and pleased with the surroundings and the majority of the property's characteristics after conducting the physical inspection, you should proceed ahead by taking legal steps, some of which are described below:

1. Hiring a Lawyer: Before you pay, you should hire a lawyer with extensive experience in property practice to perform due diligence on the property you plan to purchase and to prepare all the required paperwork. The property title may be a C of O, a deed of assignment, or a governor's consent. It is important to remember that a survey plan is simply a map that shows where the property is located and names it; if it is offered to you as a document of title, we strongly advise against accepting it.

2. Searching at the Land Registry: Your attorney would proceed to search at the state land registry or the federal land registry. If the land is state land with the governor's consent, your attorney would search the state land registry; if the land is federal land, your attorney would need to search the federal land registry. Through the search, you will be able to learn about the property's history, who owns it, its exact size, transactions on the property, whether it has been used as a mortgage or encumbered in any way, whether it has been sold or leased to some individuals in the past, and all other relevant information. Following the search, your attorney will provide you with advice regarding the real status of the property.

3. Existing Charges: You should make sure you investigate whether there are any backlogs, land-due charges, or electricity bills on the property. The owner may have neglected to pay land-due charges because he wants to sell; these are statutory fees on every property that the owner must pay annually; whatever the name in your state, it's important to find out if the owner has neglected to pay them. This does not necessarily mean the property is not a good fit for you to buy, but it will affect your negotiating position if the sellers know you plan to settle all of these bills.

4. Building Approval Document: You might want to ask for the building approval document. If the property is a house, apartment, or duplex, it wouldn't be inappropriate for you to inquire about the existence of one. This way, you can make sure that should you decide to purchase the property, you won't lose it to the government when they come to demolish it because the building approval wasn't obtained.

5. Technical Matters: Before making a purchase, you should visit the property with a technical person, such as an engineer, builder, architect, or anyone else skilled in structural or technical matters related to properties. These people can help inspect the necessary corrections and renovations as well as check the structure to ensure that the property is well-built.

6. Check for Litigation: Your lawyer can go above and beyond by visiting the high court registry to ascertain whether the property you wish to purchase is included in the list of properties that are under litigation, which would

The Law Behind Your Real Estate Portfolio

be incorrect and not in the seller's best interests. There is a where you have descriptions of properties that are under litigation, so it may be that there is a dispute on the property between parties and it is registered at the high court. If it is land, you might also wish to arrange for a land surveyor to visit to verify that the land's location corresponds with the title document that the seller has provided you. The surveyor would use a GPS device to visit the site and record the **Beacons** and **Coordinates** to verify to you that the land you have been brought to purchase is the same as the land that is listed on the survey plan that is attached to the land documents of title.

After you've completed all of these steps and your lawyer has given you the all-clear to proceed with payment, your lawyer can then draft a document of purchase. Since you are the one giving up money, you should be protected, so it is preferable if your lawyer handles this part of the process. Additionally, you should take immediate possession of the property upon payment and signing for it, as this is one of the best ways to assert ownership of the property.

Possession is very important. Leaving your land barren doesn't always make sense since it might draw in land hijackers. Although you may eventually get your property back, the stress is not worth it. If there is a third-party interest or anybody who feels you are wrong to have possessed the property, such people can show up and challenge you, and then things can be resolved as soon as possible. Additionally, once you have acquired your property, you must register your title. Some people simply purchase properties and hold onto them for a long period because they think they know the seller. This seller could be a friend, family member, or someone close to you. If the seller passes away, there may be no one to verify your account for purchasing the property. Therefore, documentation is crucial, and you must register your title with the state land registry so that the government is aware that you are the rightful owner of the land and to serve as a notice to anyone wishing to purchase or take possession of the property because your name will already be recorded as the owner of the property

Chapter Three

Recognizing Important Terms, Types, And Avoidable Pitfalls in Real Estate Contracts

Avoid getting overwhelmed by real estate contracts. Legal agreements that outline the terms and conditions of acquiring, selling, or renting a property are known as **REAL ESTATE CONTRACTS.** These agreements, which serve as the cornerstone of every real estate transaction, must be reviewed and agreed upon by both parties. Ignorance of a real estate contract may result in litigation, financial losses, and other concerns. Let's go over the numerous sorts of real estate contracts, crucial terminology, clauses to look for, and the reasons you should always have a real estate lawyer on your side for protection.

Real Estate Contract Types

There are many various sorts of real estate contracts, and each form has a specific role. The most common kinds of real estate contracts are as follows:

☐ The most typical sort of real estate transaction is the purchase agreement. It outlines all of the conditions for acquiring a house, such as the down payment amount, the closing date, and any contingencies.

☐ A listing agreement is a legal agreement that grants a real estate agent authorization to sell a property on behalf of the owner. It covers the listing price, the marketing approach, and the agent's pay.

☐ A lease agreement is a written contract that describes the terms and conditions of renting a property, including the rent amount, security deposit, and length of the lease. It is signed by a renter and a landlord.

☐ An option agreement is a legal instrument that offers a potential buyer the right to acquire real estate at a set price for a certain length of time.

Important Words and Clauses to Search For

There are various crucial terms and clauses to look for when reading a real estate contract. Among them are:

Purchase Price and Terms of Payment

Both the purchase price and the terms of payment must be specifically specified in the contract. This contains the loan requirements, closing charges, and the amount of the down payment.

Property Description and Conditions

A full description of the property, including its location, size, and status, should be included in the contract. Include a clear description of any problems or remedies that are necessary.

Contingencies and Conditions

These are prerequisites that need to be met, such as a successful inspection or the buyer's ability to secure financing, for the deal to continue.

Disclosures and Warranties

Any known faults or concerns with the property must be reported by the seller. Other guarantees, like a builder's warranty or a home warranty, might also be included.

Closing date date date and location

The contract should make clear the closure date and location.

Typical Errors to Steer Clear Of

Avoiding common dangers is vital when signing a real estate contract.

➤ *Not giving the material a serious reading*

It's crucial to thoroughly review the contract and make sure you grasp all of the terms and conditions.

➢ *Unwilling to negotiate for terms and conditions*

Before you sign the contract, you should consider the terms and situations that work best for you.

➢ *Relying mainly on promises made orally*

Legally, verbal agreements are not enforceable. Make sure every agreement is contained in the contract and established in writing.

The Law Behind Your Real Estate Portfolio

Strategies for Bargaining with Tenants on Lease Terms

It may be tough to design a lease that works for both landlords and tenants and is affordable. Conditions that you may think acceptable may not be what a tenant is seeking in a rental house. However, you may be willing to work out a lease with them if they're a decent tenant with an immaculate rental history. We'll explore how to design a reasonable lease agreement, some lease terms to consider when when when negotiating, and tips for landlords throughout the negotiation process today.

Is it possible to discuss lease terms with tenants?

Indeed, it's more common than you may imagine to discuss lease requirements with tenants. While many lease requirements are carved in stone and cannot be modified, others might be negotiable. It's vital to learn how to negotiate with tenants. Tenants typically want to argue over the amount of the security deposit or the rental charge. A lease may, nevertheless, be feasible to agree on in various scenarios.

Conditions You Could Be Willing to Bargain

Even though you may believe you have a faultless lease agreement, your tenants may not agree. They might therefore contact you with inquiries or counteroffers on particular lease terms. You might be willing to negotiate these criteria with tenants.

Rent Amount

Your tenant might approach you and seek a decreased monthly rent payment. Nevertheless, it might be good to bargain, especially if your tenant is willing to sign a longer lease, has an outstanding rental history, or is in charge of specific maintenance chores.

Lease-term negotiations

Length of Lease: While you may opt for longer-term commitments for stability, some tenants might prefer a shorter lease time for flexibility. Nevertheless, it's vital to create a solution that appeases both parties.

Security Deposit: Although there may be some freedom in this, security deposits are commonly set by the monthly rent. For example, you may consider waiving the deposit for tenants who have a clean credit record or a great rental history.

Pet Policies: If your property has a no-pet policy, tenants may barter for the opportunity to bring their pets, provided that they agree to pay for any damages or an additional pet fee.

Options for Renewal: The terms of the lease renewal, including the possibility of a rent increase, may be discussed. Tenants who are trustworthy and reliable may negotiate acceptable renewal circumstances and sign a new lease without paying extra money.

How to Write Terms of Lease That Are Fair to Both Parties

Flexible lease durations that are based on market research are vital. To make sure the terms of the lease are appropriate for both parties, landlords must undertake the required research. You should also be adaptive and willing to work out a deal on unique leasing terms with respectable tenants. Here's how to design fair lease clauses that benefit both landlords and tenants.

- ★ Recognize the requirements of both parties
- ★ Examine markets prices
- ★ Emphasize Your Tenant's Duties
- ★ Talk about rental increases
- ★ Consult a lawyer

Recognize the requirements of both parties

Contracts between landlords and tenants that are legally binding are called lease agreements. It is consequently in your best interest to add requirements and standards for renters that secure both you and your property. On the other hand, you should also consider your tenants' requests. Seek information from prior renters on what worked and what may be improved about renting from you to get a better idea of the lease terms that future tenants are searching for.

Examine market prices

Without an understanding of the rental market, it is impossible to create a suitable lease agreement. You want to know what your property is worth, how it compares against other homes in the community, and the normal rental rates, after all. Take into consideration your location, the amenities you provide, and the size of your property. You may establish a fair yet competitive rental cost with the assistance of these factors.

Emphasize Your Tenant's Duties

It is crucial that your lease agreement precisely explains the duties of the tenant. Ignoring who is in charge could result in misunderstandings and possibly harm to your property. To prevent small issues from turning into large ones, establish a communication system for reporting maintenance concerns as soon as feasible. Tenants should also be made aware of their obligations concerning disposing of rubbish, obeying community norms, and informing them of any changes in occupancy.

Talk About A Rental Increase

It's vital to be transparent and honest in your contract if you wish to increase the rent at any moment during the lease term or at the time of renewal. If this is your approach, offer proof of property enhancements, additional running expenditures, or new features to back any recommended raises. For tenants' advantage, you may even consider extending a longer lease term, which may help mitigate the consequences of annual rises. Furthermore, maintain an open mind when it comes to negotiating rent rises in light of factors like regular rent payments, a strong rental history, or extended lease responsibilities.

Consult a lawyer

Given that leases are legally binding contracts, you should make sure yours abides by all relevant local, state, and federal requirements by consulting with an attorney. It's also vital to keep up with any alterations or changes to the legislation in your jurisdiction that might influence the terms of your lease. It's necessary to have a legal structure in your lease contract that defends the rights and interests of both parties and manages circumstances like lease terminations, eviction proceedings, and dispute resolution. Provide a copy of the lease and any other important paperwork to tenants in the case of legal difficulty, and advise them to seek an attorney.

Strategies For Bargaining With Tenants On Lease Terms

It's vital to be ready to handle any questions, concerns, or negotiations a tenant may have regarding the lease you issued. You don't want to reject adjustments or shut them off immediately. Rather, engage the topic with an open mind. These are some ideas for deciding on lease terms with tenants.

Communicate Clearly: When using legal lease or complicated vocabulary in discussions, try to avoid adding extra complications to the matter.

Rather, express the terms of the lease simply and understandably to all parties.

Be Open to Change: Have an open mind before going into negotiations. Be receptive to tenant recommendations that vary from your own, especially if they have well-reasoned needs.

Engage in Person Negotiations: These give rapid replies to issues and concerns as well as explanations. This may ensure a more effective bargaining process and assist in the prompt settlement of difficulties. Show compassion by recognizing and respecting the specific circumstances that your tenants are experiencing. For example, to establish a more cooperative atmosphere during conversations, treat people with understanding if they are going through personal challenges.

Keep Records of Everything: Make sure the lease terms you settle upon are explicit and devoid of any potential for interpretation. All established agreements, including any amendments or special arrangements, must be documented. Property management may assist in securing fair lease conditions.

One of the most crucial components of being a landlord or property manager is understanding how to conduct tenant conversations. It's vital to preserve consistency and justice while considering the law and the interests of both parties into consideration.

OWNERSHIP OF PROPERTY

Assume you are a resident of an area where the water you drink is polluted by factory pollutants. The firm does not care whether or not it contaminates the water, as it owns property rights to the land. But what if it were conceived of as your property right to use clean, drinking water? The firm would then be worried about whether or not it taints the water.

A bundle of regulations known as property rights specifies what individuals and organizations are authorized to do with their property. Property rights give you the flexibility to develop and sell the land you own. They also restrict other parties from utilizing your land for reasons other than those approved by you. A bundle of laws known as property rights outlines what a person or organization is entitled to do with their property. Government-outlined laws and regulations will rigorously protect and preserve the property rights of people or corporations. These rules and regulations not only define and explain property ownership but also preserve any benefits that come with being the legitimate owner of the item. For instance, property rights rules and regulations ensure that you get paid each month if you opt to rent out your dwelling as an owner. It's vital to note that the word "property" may signify many distinct things. When we speak about property, we're not just talking about vehicles or real estate; we're also talking about patents that someone may hold on to their ideas. Nonetheless, there may be considerable national disparities in the extent of legal protection granted to some property rights.

In countries where the state maintains a legal framework that awards and preserves property rights, people may only gain property rights via transactions that have been mutually agreed upon. For instance, when someone voluntarily contributes to a charity or distributes their inheritance, the receiver of these activities only becomes the owner of the given property with the approval of both parties. Furthermore, when two individuals agree to a transaction, the other person gains ownership of the property while selling a dwelling. Even if the tenant is utilizing the premises, the property owner still retains ownership rights if they rent out their rental property to a renter.

Conversely, some governments give their citizens limited or no property rights. In regime systems like these, the government in countries and places devoid of private property rights generally distributes ownership of resources and the right to utilize them by compulsion. These countries' governments pick who is permitted to utilize the property, who is not, and who gets money from it. Economic resources are not allocated as efficiently when property rights are gone, which has different harmful externalities that impact individuals and organizations.

Externalities of Property Rights

There are externalities associated with property rights in every business transaction. Externalities are the positive or negative external effects that an organization or individual has on other parties as a result of their activities.

For instance, you are negatively impacted by a company's commercial activities if you reside next to a factory whose output poisons the water. This is because it contaminates the water you drink, enhancing the likelihood of sickness. Positive and negative externalities are shared more efficiently when the government makes it obvious what each party's property rights are. To be defined as an externality, however, there must be a measurable economic consequence brought about by the person or the firm. Fossil fuel power plants generate reactive and hazardous compounds, making them a significant source of industrial effluent. Dumping garbage into bodies or into bodies of water without following correct treatment and management methods may have harmful health implications. This has adverse implications for the local inhabitants as well as the surroundings. Fossil fuel power stations may continue functioning due to property rights. But what about the folks who dwell in the neighborhood? Drinkable water would be regarded as a property right in a system where property rights are comprehensive and well-defined, taking into consideration the expenses that people endure as a consequence of fossil fuel power plants. That is to say, individuals have the property right to drink clean water, just as the fossil fuel power plant has the right to conduct business. Under such situations, the government mandates the enterprise to manage water resources in a way that minimizes pollution of the water supply. Reducing water contamination will come at an added expense to the firm. The increased expenditure for the firm is nearly comparable to what individuals pay as a consequence of dirty water. On the other side, the complete negative externality of the company's property right to conduct business would fall upon the people if they did not have access to drinking water, which is a property right, in the area of the fossil-fuel power plant. When certain resources lack well-defined property rights, both positive and negative externalities may develop. Put simply, a transaction may only transmit a benefit or impose a cost on other parties without compensating them if the rights to particular resources are still up for dispute. This is the one case where this is conceivable. For example, there is a lack of clarity on the right to breathe clean air, which contributes to the external costs connected with automobile emissions.

Externalities relating to property rights

Remedies

Property rights externalities may be mitigated by people or corporations via talks or by bringing a lawsuit for damages.

Bargaining

Property rights owners are receptive to talks and negotiations on behalf of people or firms that are badly harmed by property rights externalities. They may agree to pay a fraction of the expenses connected with the adverse externality. The negotiation technique shouldn't be expensive for the bargaining solution to be successful. Regardless of how property rights are established, an effective solution will be achieved when parties can negotiate without spending money and to their mutual benefit. However, negotiation may be expensive and time-consuming, particularly when there are no established property rights. Furthermore, the negotiation process becomes considerably more complex when several parties are influenced by the externalities of property rights.

Filing a damage lawsuit

An injured party has the legal right to sue the other party liable for the negative externality when it is caused by that party. The victim may be entitled to financial restitution for their expenditures if their claim is validated in court.

Property rights are important

Property rights are vital because they ensure the economy's effective use of resources and the elimination of undesirable externalities that damage people and other enterprises. The safety of the water we drink or the purity of the air we breathe cannot be guaranteed by the free market. Rather, communities depend on their governments to conserve the environment and adopt regulations that insulate them from the harmful impacts of property rights. The market is unable to allocate resources, which is why the air we breathe is toxic or the water is polluted. Property rights are, after all, insufficiently and ineffectively established. The government can stop many of the harmful repercussions of air pollution and water contamination by protecting property rights that ensure everyone has access to clean water and air. A classic example would be the sale of pollution permits, which would incentivize industries to limit air pollution. This is because the corporation would suffer expenditures as a consequence of air pollution.

The death rate would drop as a result of decreased air pollution. More healthy individuals could contribute to the labor force and enhance the GDP of the nation. The gain from the government selling pollution permits would be significantly greater than the expenditure on them, which is a firm facing increasing production expenses. Property rights are crucial in dispersing resources in an economy much more efficiently.

Characteristics of Property Rights

The aspects of property rights establish an owner's rights, privileges, and constraints on resource utilization. Property rights are defined by three main factors:

Exclusiveness

The right to exclusivity assures that the owner of the property pays all expenditures and rewards related to that privilege. In other words, the holder of a property right needs to avoid producing externalities.

Transferability

Another key component of property rights is transferability, which permits individuals to give ownership to other people. It is subject to the necessity that the transfer of ownership of the property rights be authorized by both parties.

Enforceability

Enforceability provides that the holding of property rights, as well as the transfer of them, is done in a legally binding fashion. Property rights prohibit others from taking ownership of or invading your property.

Different property rights

Private, common, and public property are the three basic forms of property rights. Individuals with private property rights are awarded ownership of particular property and have the capacity to prohibit others from benefiting from it.

When someone possesses private property, they have the authority to block other individuals from exploiting or benefiting from their assets.

A single person, a group of individuals, a firm, or an organization that may be given private property rights but does not benefit from its activities can all be referred to as persons.

Property rights that are owned and managed collectively are referred to as common property. Examples of this form of property right include grazing rights on public lands and open ocean fishing. Because diverse parties will disagree on how best to handle these resources, common property legislation may be quite problematic.

State property is another term for public property. Even though this form of property belongs to all citizens, it is controlled by the government.

A location that is controlled by the state is a **national park**.

Chapter 4

What Does Joint Tenancy Mean When Owning Property?

A legal arrangement known as a "**joint tenancy**" is one in which two or more persons jointly hold a piece of property and have equal rights and duties. Friends, relatives, business colleagues, and married or single couples may all create joint tenancies. This legal arrangement provides a right of survivorship, which implies that in the case of an owner's death, the surviving party or parties will instantly receive the property without going through probate or court procedures. A sort of property ownership typically associated with real estate is joint tenancy. In a shared tenancy, each individual has an equal interest in the property, including any financial burdens and rewards. A right of survivorship is formed by a joint tenancy, meaning that the interest of the dead party instantly goes to the surviving tenant or tenants.

A tenancy in common, in which the portion of a deceased tenant is handed to their heirs, is not the same as a joint tenancy. Without the other tenants' approval, one tenant may unilaterally dissolve a joint tenancy.

THE OPERATION OF JOINT TENANCY

A sort of property ownership typically associated with real estate is joint tenancy. Through the use of a deed, two or more parties come together at the same time to form a binding legal agreement. These folks could be friends, relatives, or even colleagues. Assume, for illustrative purposes, that a single couple buys a property. When they acquired the home, they chose a shared tenancy. The two owners will be designated as joint tenants on the property's deed. Each party participates in the benefits since they each have a claim to the property. Each partner is entitled to 50% of the proceeds if they desire to sell the property or rent it out to another individual. However, because of their partnership, they share equal financial responsibility for the house's maintenance, taxes, and mortgage. The other party is required to suffer the repercussions if one does not meet their financial obligations.

Survivorship Rights

Additionally, this agreement provides a right of survivorship. This means that the other party will instantly become the entire owner of the property upon the death of the first. Probate and the transfer of a deceased person's assets to an estate are no longer required as a consequence. Probate courts decide if a person's will is authentic and divide assets among the deceased's dependents in an appropriate way. Joint tenancy with the right of survivorship is a legal concept that may be utilized for several assets, including brokerage accounts and companies, even though it is most closely associated with real estate ownership. Tenancy has a strong association with real estate because it's generally considered to signify owning or living in a home. Since a joint tenancy creates a right of survivorship, the property does not need to go through the probate procedure.

Establishing Joint Tenancy

In most instances, establishing a joint tenancy needs the existence of four elements. Keep in mind that not all legal systems may require them, and there may be extra prerequisites in specific cases before a joint tenancy may be created. The four notions revolve around possession, interest, title, and time.

Time

Usually, the necessity for time implies that each joint renter must obtain their ownership interest in the property at the same time. Joint tenants should acquire their rights in the property from the same event, even if they do not need to sign the same document at the same time. The unity of time is satisfied, for instance, if two individuals jointly acquire a piece of real estate and both names appear on the same deed with the same date. Keep in mind that alterations to the ownership structure are usual as ownership expands. For instance, if the two quit being friends, then one of them give up ownership or be replaced by a new co-owner? In general, shared tenancy occurs naturally from the outset of an ownership structure, yet it may evolve.

Title

All joint tenants must receive their ownership rights via the same legal instrument or document, according to the title. This effectively indicates that co-owners should be registered on the same deed or other necessary legal paperwork if two or more persons are acquiring a property jointly. Joint tenancy is legitimate, for example, if three persons are specified as joint tenants in a single deed transferring the property to them. For authentic ownership status to be preserved, this criterion is needed. It could be difficult or ineffectual to identify who owns a property and when their ownership began if there are several ownership paperwork. Furthermore, in the event of financial hardship, each joint owner must be recognized exactly because they share similar financial interests in a piece of property.

Interest

The split of property among joint owners is referred to as interest. A joint tenant's equal and undivided portion of the property is guaranteed by interest. This signifies that each co-owner owns the same amount of the firm. For instance, each joint tenant would possess 50% of the property in a joint tenancy involving two persons. Each joint tenant would possess 33.33% of the property in a joint tenancy with three persons, and so on. Owner interest is not necessarily equal or fair in other kinds of legal ownership. Unless otherwise indicated and agreed upon by all parties, each joint owner will normally have an equal share in most real estate transactions.

Possession

The word "*possession*" refers to the equal right of each joint tenant to use and possess the entire property. It means that no co-tenant may claim exclusive control over any specific piece of the property. Rather, the complete property may be accessed and utilized by each co-owner. This principle sets joint tenancy different from other kinds of co-ownership, such as tenancy in common, in which each co-owner may hold separate, autonomous pieces of the property. Furthermore, it enhances the property's liability in the case of an emergency. For instance, all joint owners are generally accountable for paying for major water damage that happens in a single room (ignoring any specific grounds for damage or separate agreements).

The Financial Effects of Co-Tenancy

When it comes to property ownership, joint tenancy involves numerous distinct financial concerns. Because joint tenants own an equal amount of the property, all co-owners share an equal financial burden and benefit. They also divide the expenses of closing charges, down payments, and other connected expenditures when purchasing a property. Joint owners are jointly accountable for keeping up a strong credit score and making mortgage payments after the closing. Regardless of individual contributions, all co-owners share the same amount of property taxes. All joint owners must equally divide the expenses of maintenance and repairs, make decisions on upgrades and repairs collectively, and split the expenditures equally. According to the percentages of ownership interests held by each joint tenant, revenue from the property should be paid equally to each renter. Furthermore, if the property is sold, profits (and the accompanying capital gains taxes) might be applicable; the tax repercussions would vary depending on local legislation, the term of ownership, and the part of the property owned by each joint tenant.

Breaking Up a Joint Tenancy

In terms of property ownership, there are various methods to dissolve a shared tenancy. If all joint tenants agree willingly, they may cancel the joint tenancy and establish a tenancy in common, generally by written contract or agreement. This voluntary agreement typically finds hurdles and may not be able to be entirely carried out if all parties are in dispute. A joint tenant's piece of the property may be sold or transferred to a third party via **conveyance**, making that person a tenant in common with the current joint tenants. Certain issues may develop when the present tenants examine or approve the new owner (taking into account big sports teams that are subject to severe ownership requirements and a thorough review system, for example). A court may order an involuntary severance in specified cases, and partition proceedings are costly and time-consuming legal procedures. Conflicting interests or arguments amongst the joint tenants may be the cause of this.

Benefits and Drawbacks of Co-Tenancy

While there are numerous advantages to joint tenancy, there are also some evident negatives that should be taken into mind before signing the agreement.

Benefits of Co-Tenancy

As previously indicated, it removes the problems of settling the property via an estate via a will, provided that one co-tenant survives.

- When someone dies away, their will normally go through probate, a legal process where the courts analyze the will to confirm it is valid. Normally, if someone dies away, the survivor cannot access or claim their assets until they are released by probate.

- If a deceased person leaves no will or beneficiary designations, the probate system also assists in establishing how their assets are split. But it may easily take months to conclude the process. By skipping probate and the drawn-out legal process, a joint tenancy allows the joint tenant to acquire rapid ownership of the assets.

- Every member of a shared tenancy has responsibility for the property in addition to enjoying its perks. For instance, one spouse cannot take out a mortgage loan on the property and leave the other accountable for the debt. If a loan is taken out on the property, all parties are answerable for the debt as the joint tenancy includes both assets and responsibilities.

Drawbacks of Co-Tenancy

- Divorce and other marital troubles could make co-tenancy more challenging.

- As previously noted, neither party may sell any jointly owned assets without the other's agreement. Additionally, both partners are the proprietors of any debts.

- The administration of the asset, if one or more of the joint tenants die away, is yet another negative of joint tenancy. Because joint tenancy affords the survivor all the rights, the survivor is not legally compelled to execute the deceased's request to pass the property's value to named heirs.

- Advantages When a tenant in a shared tenancy dies away, probate court is avoided.

- The joint tenant inherits everything immediately away, even in the absence of a will or beneficiaries mentioned.

Cons

- Since both tenants must approve, marital troubles may make the sale of assets more complex and take longer.

- All assets in a joint tenancy belong to the partner; the deceased cannot leave assets to their heirs.

Separate Tenancy vs. Common Tenancy

Certain joint owners select tenancy in common (JTIC) over joint tenancy to keep control over how the property is allocated after their deaths. Percentage-based ownership is conceivable with tenancy in common since shares may be transferred and new tenants may be added at any moment during the agreement's life rather than just at its inception. To put it another way, unlike in a joint tenancy, where assets automatically pass to the surviving partner upon death, in a tenancy in common, the assets may be allocated by the conditions provided in the decedent's will and local laws.

Explain the meaning of "joint tenancy with right of survivorship."

Each owner has equal rights over a piece of property under a joint tenancy with the right of survivorship. The other joint tenants acquire the property's portion in the case of one of the owners' deaths rather than having it probated with their inheritance.

How many joint tenants are authorized in one piece of real estate?

There may be two or more joint tenants in a joint tenancy. In a joint tenancy, the number of co-owners is limitless as long as each joint tenant owns an equal piece of the firm.

What Would Happen if One Joint Tenant Quits Paying the Property's Bills?

According to their ownership share, each joint tenant is legally compelled to contribute a portion of the property's costs, including maintenance, property taxes, and mortgage payments. The other joint tenants may be obliged to pay their portion to avert default or other financial troubles if one of them stops paying payments. Legal action might be necessary to enforce the co-ownership agreement if problems emerge.

Can New Co-Owners Be Added to the Property by Joint Tenants?

In general, all joint tenants must buy their shares concurrently for a joint tenancy to occur. A tenancy in common rather than a joint tenancy would presumably be developed if other co-owners were joined after the initial transaction. Joint tenants may, however, sell or transfer their shares, and this technique may be utilized to add new co-owners.

Is it Possible for Debtors to Sue the Property to Recover Debts from a Single Joint Tenant?

Yes, creditors may seek to construct a lien on the property or force the sale of the property to reclaim the remaining sum if one joint tenant has personal debts or judgments. The other joint tenants and the property's status as a joint tenancy may be influenced by the creditor's action.

Conclusion

A basic legal mechanism for two or more persons to share equal interests in real estate or other forms of property is via joint tenancy. It is not essential to probate a tenant's part of the property with their estate when they die away. Rather, it is only the remaining joint tenants who collect the deceased tenant's portion.

Chapter Five

Zoning Laws

An Overview Of How They Affect Property Development

Every investor, especially one running a real estate investment firm, should be educated about zoning restrictions as they are a vital component of real estate development. These policies have a direct influence on property development and use, and they are vital in defining how a community is set out. We will discuss zoning restrictions, their relevance, and their possible influence on real estate development in this chapter.

Do Zoning Laws Exist?

Local governments implement zoning laws, usually referred to as zoning ordinances or rules, to limit land use within specified zones. Ensuring orderly and proper land development while improving the general welfare, safety, and health of a community is the basic purpose of zoning laws.

Zoning's Effect on Real Estate Development

Land Use Types: Zoning restrictions frequently define zones or districts, each of which is confined to a set of permissible land uses. Commercial, industrial, residential, and agricultural are examples of frequent zoning categories. Knowing these categories is vital for a real estate investment business when analyzing probable investment properties. It is crucial to know what sorts of projects are authorized in a specific place and whether or not they fit in with your investment strategy. Within a given zone, property density is also limited by property density zoning. It specifies criteria for things like building height, lot size, and the number of dwellings per acre. The feasibility and profitability of your real estate holdings may be greatly influenced by these restrictions.

Building rules and setbacks: Zoning laws frequently define setbacks or the required separations between a building and nearby structures or property boundaries. They may also define design standards and building guidelines, which influence a property's appearance and function. Real estate developers must abide by certain guidelines.

Conditional Use Permits: Occasionally, you may wish to employ a piece of property for anything other than what its zoning category permits. Conditional use permits are important in this circumstance. Comprehending the technique for gaining these permits is vital if you're thinking about building an uncommon or distinctive piece of property.

In summary

Zoning restrictions are a significant issue in the world of real estate investment when analyzing properties. They may drastically affect the success of your investment and directly affect what you may do with a property. To effectively handle the difficult world of zoning laws, it's vital to learn about and grasp local zoning limits, interact with local authorities, and, if needed, acquire legal help. By doing this, you can check that your projects are by the development goals of the local community and make well-informed investment decisions.

Environmental Law and Transactions in Real Estate

The purpose of environmental law is to defend the environment from damage and degradation brought about by human activities. Its fundamental purpose is to assist sustainable development while assuring a secure and healthy environment for all living beings. However, what relevance does this have to real estate deals? Environmental law is crucial to all real estate transactions in various ways. For example, rules limiting the disposal of hazardous waste are scrupulously adhered to. By guaranteeing that any property involved in a transaction is free of hazardous waste, these restrictions safeguard the environment and public health. The severe repercussions of disobedience underline how crucial it is for both customers and sellers to adhere to these standards.Furthermore, development is restricted in ecologically vulnerable regions like wetlands or endangered species' habitats under environmental standards. In this scenario, the law seeks to conserve these critical ecosystems and requires that landowners first secure the proper approvals before initiating any development activities. Both parties in a transaction need to grasp and abide by these constraints. Real estate agreements may also be severely influenced by lawsuits concerning environmental hazards. For instance, a property's participation in polluted soil or environmental difficulties may cause the sale or purchase process to be delayed or even derailed. If a transaction entails prospective environmental liabilities, buyers might be reluctant to move ahead, and sellers would need to take care of these difficulties before concluding the purchase. This brings up the topic of buyers' and sellers' legal duties. To uncover probable threats, purchasers are expected to perform comprehensive due diligence, which includes environmental site investigations. Conversely, sellers are obligated to warn the buyer of any known environmental dangers. A smooth transaction may be secured and future difficulties may be avoided with open communication and openness.

Handling Environmental Difficulties in Real Estate Deals

So how can we overcome these challenges relating to the environment to make sure that real estate sales run well? To detect any environmental risks, undertake extensive environmental due diligence, which includes site studies and historical background checks.

Seek professional advice: To manage intricate requirements, work with environmental attorneys who are skilled in environmental law.

Obtain the essential permissions: Before commencing construction, verify sure you have the necessary permits if your property is situated in an ecologically sensitive region.

contract with environmental challenges as quickly as possible: Before concluding the contract, eliminate any environmental hazards or work out acceptable terms.

Remain Informed: Environmental laws are subject to regular revisions. To make sure you're continually in compliance, acquire legal assistance.

Speak with an Attorney with Experience: Environmental law is an important component of real estate negotiations, not merely an afterthought. Understanding its relevance and adhering to the laws will assist us in ensuring effective transactions that safeguard the public's health and the environment.

Important Steps to Finish the Title Search Procedure

Title Lookup

A title search, also known as a property title search, is a technique used in real estate law to gather documents. Determining relevant interests in the property and associated rules could be facilitated by it. To uncover the answers to these inquiries concerning a property that is for sale, a title search is frequently carried out. Does the owner of the property possess a sellable share in it? What sorts of land use permits and constraints are in

place? Does the property have any liens on it? There are two major types of title searching: a full coverage search and a limited coverage search. Non-insured reports and foreclosure guarantee searches are two more kinds. To execute a title search, clients typically elect to employ the aid of a title search business or competent attorney. completing a title search requires analyzing official land records and completing online legal research. Every record is a piece of paper that may be used as documentation of a previous incident. By uncovering any unsettled claims, the title search's ultimate purpose is to generate a unique, marketable title.

Crucial Phases in the Title Search Procedure

Locating Earlier Titles

It's the sequence in which the historical transfers of the title occur. Here, the chain contains facts on the first owner, the current owner, and any former owners of the property. Typically, public records stored in local government offices—like the County Clerk's office—are where this information is found. There needs to be a cloud on the title if this chain is not complete. This cloud in this case shows that the owner at present lacks a marketable title. There are a few plausible explanations for this chain's incompleteness. For instance, the preceding owner may have gotten the title under a different name as a consequence of deed fraud.

Title Lookup

Such situations warrant launching a lawsuit. By this, potential claimants must appear in court and give evidence that they are the true owners. They will not be authorized to express any interest in the property if they are unable to present proof of the title.

Tax Lookup

The following stage requires providing the most current tax status of the property. This is a crucial step as it enables you to find out if the property's real estate taxes have been paid in full or not. If not, how many taxes—and from how many preceding years—are unpaid and due? No one wants to acquire real estate that has unpaid taxes on it as it will result in a lien being put on it. If one of these properties is acquired, the government is authorized to put it for sale to recuperate those taxes. Additionally, be aware that, as a lender, you may secure your property from being lost due to delinquent taxes by getting it insured.

Site Examining

It is an exceedingly significant step in the title search operation. Any encroachments or other analogous concerns that might impact the title are mentioned in a report that is written by an inspection officer or inspector. In addition, they physically evaluate the property to validate its size and areas specified for renovation as well as to seek any evidence of unregistered easements. Additionally, they will examine if the property is inhabited or unoccupied. The inspector will record and transmit any factual information concerning the title, such as an unregistered easement, to the potential buyer. This step's major purpose is to obtain more data and supporting documents that will increase the authenticity of the information gathered from the title search overall.

Search by Name and Judgment

As the name indicates, judgment search is the process of identifying judgments that are pending execution by the property's owner. A judgment is a wide lien on property in real estate law. It acts as security for any outstanding debt under the judgment, which the government may sell to satisfy its expenditures. These rights belong to the government because of liens, unpaid property taxes, and court decrees. The government's rights to the property will legally take priority over those of the buyer or lender.

Before releasing the title to a buyer, the owner should rectify any title faults detected if the expert undertaking the title search discovers judgments indicating the property has a defect. To get the title released from all judgments and claims, there will be some court actions and fees required.

Finishing

A property has a lien or judgment, and the title search method typically equates to a clear selling agreement. Both parties may continue ahead with concluding the transaction if the title is clear and the problems (discovered during the search) are corrected. At that moment, the title is transferred.

In summary

By executing these procedures, one may make sure that the title is free of claims and free of faults. The conclusion of the agreement between the two parties happens more smoothly as a consequence. Because it demands substantial time and financial expenditure, the title search is also a vital aspect of the mortgage processing method. Real estate businesses, banks, and financiers commonly depend on lawyers for this.

This is due to their desire to ensure that the data they have gathered is exact and well-explained. Law businesses, in addition to bankers and real estate brokers, engage outside help for related activities like analyzing legal papers. The whole load of the law business may be eased by having an additional resource accessible when required. The internal staff may now focus on their core tasks.

Chapter Six

Techniques For Asset Protection

Professionals, business owners, investors, and others with substantial assets may all benefit from asset protection measures as they shield against *litigation, creditor claims, and other possible losses*. To safeguard assets from claims made against the owner, this generally means transferring ownership of the assets to numerous legal organizations.

Asset protection may be an essential component of a financial plan, even if it's not always straightforward, reasonable, or guaranteed to block all claims. Finding the assets and techniques that are ideal for your situation could be supported by a financial consultant.

The Law Behind Your Real Estate Portfolio

Asset Protection

What Is It?

Asset protection is the legal name for a series of tactics used to cover a person's or company's assets from demands made by creditors, tax agencies, and lawsuits. If a motorist is determined to be at fault in a vehicle accident resulting in harm, for example, these strategies may reduce the amount of money that the driver may forfeit. The greatest candidates for asset protection are individuals with large assets.

Here, occupation is also important. Owners of enterprises are among those most likely to face lawsuits for damages, especially those who employ workers. Real estate speculators and highly rewarded medical practitioners, notably surgeons and obstetricians, are among the others at risk. Additionally, asset preservation may protect assets from being lost in a *divorce*. **_In that perspective, everyone who is married may be a prospective asset projection candidate._** Although beneficial, asset protection has its limitations. For people with little or no assets, it may incur enormous expenditures and complexity and be of reduced relevance.

Furthermore, asset protection is not impervious to all taxes or other sorts of liens, including mechanical liens.

Techniques for the Protection of Assets

The protection of assets is very **individualized**. It is quite likely that any asset protection strategy will differ from all or the majority of previous asset protection strategies in a few most important areas. In spite of this, there is a restricted selection of instruments that may be used. The following are some of the techniques that are most important:

- ❖ Take charge after a lawsuit has been filed or a tax liability has been assessed, it is often too late to make an effort to salvage assets. To get the best possible results, asset protection should be put into place before the need arises. It is common practice to employ a limited liability company (LLC) as an asset protection vehicle since it is uncomplicated, cost-effective, and extensively used. It is possible to shield assets such as real estate, vehicles, and other assets from lawsuits and other claims that are made against the owners of the limited liability company (LLC) by creating an LLC and transferring them into the LLC. The avoidance of double taxation on firm revenue is another method LLCs could manage taxes. Irrevocable trusts known as asset protection trusts offer safe havens for assets taken out of the original owner's hands. Assets transferred into an asset protection trust are frequently safeguarded from litigation and creditor claims filed against a person or corporation. Owners may designate themselves as general partners of partnerships that contain assets they wish to keep secure via family-limited partnerships. One may form limited partners out of family members. This is a sensible method of estate tax management. Another option to make succession easier is to establish tenancy by the entirety, which retains shared ownership and survivor benefits while insulating assets from certain creditors and legal action. It is a form of shared ownership between spouses in a marriage.

❖ Retirement funds are typically shielded from bankruptcy under federal law and give considerable tax advantages. Additionally, they might be shielded from the lawsuit and debt-related claims, but, state legislation on this varies.

❖ One crucial technique for securing assets is insurance. The insurance company, not the policyholder, pays the claim when someone is wounded at home or work and their liability insurance covers it. Life insurance may ensure survivors' financial stability, and policies with rising cash value may also be sheltered from creditor claims.

States have various laws safeguarding annuities from creditors and other claims. Certain states grant no protection at all, while others merely offer limited protection, and still others offer comprehensive protection.

State laws generally safeguard homesteads. There are huge variances in the degree of protection granted by states; some do not protect at all, while others safeguard an unlimited amount of home equity from litigation.

- ❖ Another crucial element for avoiding lawsuit-related losses is discretion. People who conduct lifestyles that create the appearance that they have great money are more likely to become the subject of torts and other legal proceedings.

In summary

Asset protection measures may insulate persons and corporations from monetary losses brought on by lawsuit judgments, creditor claims, and certain taxes. Generally speaking, asset protection means transferring ownership of assets from a person or organization to a distinct legal authority. Although asset protection measures may be expensive and ongoing, and they may not always be able to shield all assets against all claims, they are nevertheless a significant component of many financial plans.

The Law Behind Your Real Estate Portfolio

Advice for Safeguarding Assets

You may evaluate what needs to be secured and how best to achieve so with the advice of a financial professional. It is not difficult to locate a professional financial consultant. You may interview each advisor match at no cost to select which one is ideal for you. Get begun right away if you're prepared to engage an advisor who can aid you in accomplishing your financial ambitions. Transferring assets to an offshore asset protection trust created in a nation like the Cook Islands or Nevis may enable you to preserve them after a lawsuit is filed, even though asset protection is frequently something you need to have in place before you need it. The jurisdiction of US courts is not recognized in these countries. Domestic asset protection trusts, however, normally need to be founded and funded long in advance of any possible need.

How to resolve disputes concerning borders

In England, property owners may face a considerable lot of stress owing to legal boundary disputes, which frequently result in strained relationships and costly court confrontations. These issues may emerge when nearby landowners disagree or cannot agree on the exact location of a property's boundary. Nonetheless, there are various methods to resolve these disagreements outside of court and avert drawn-out legal processes.

Recognizing the Conflict

Diverse circumstances could give rise to boundary disputes, including incorrect property descriptions, changes in land usage over time, or fundamental miscommunications among neighbors. Before trying any form of dispute mediation, it is vital to establish the fundamental basis for the disagreement.

Solutions for the Situation

The following are your major choices for settling a border dispute:

1. Interaction and Conciliation

The first step in addressing a border problem between neighbors is generally to have an open and honest talk. Finding common ground and feasible ideas may be aided by having a calm and constructive talk. A non-confrontational option called mediation is provided if direct contact proves to be challenging. In this case, a neutral third person may bring the parties toward a mutually agreed decision by fostering talks.

2. Expert Surveys

A detailed property survey completed by a qualified surveyor is frequently viewed as a crucial first step in resolving boundary disputes. To exactly establish the borders, a surveyor will assess physical markers, historical documents, and other essential information. The following surveyor's report may assist in resolving the argument. Expert witness reports that are well prepared could be used in court as evidence that the judge approves of them.

3. Boundary Consent

The parties involved may sign a boundary agreement when the boundaries have been accurately identified by a survey. The agreed-upon property borders and any unique requirements for land use or care are mentioned in this legal document. A border agreement may contribute to preventing future disputes by establishing a definite point of reference for the future.

4. Act of Correction

A document of rectification might be necessary if inaccuracies in property deeds are the cause of the border dispute. This legal document guarantees that the property borders are accurately described by rectifying any inaccuracies or omissions in the deed. In USA, settling legal boundary disputes relies on a combination of professional expertise, skilled communication, and a willingness to explore different routes to resolution. By adopting proactive actions like contracting with a surveyor and drafting boundary agreements, problems may be averted before they become drawn out and costly court battles. Using nonviolent tactics, such as mediation, enhances neighborly relationships. To ensure that boundary disputes are handled fairly and effectively, property owners in England need to appreciate the essence of the issue and hunt for cooperative options.

What Constitutes a Real Estate Contract Breach?

A lawful contract is broken when one of the parties **doesn't** perform what they are meant to, which is termed a **breach of contract**. The stipulations of a contract serve as a guide for the parties as to what must be done and how for them to maintain their promise. The non-breaching party may be allowed to sue the other party in court if the other party breaches the conditions of the agreement. There are two sorts of contract breaches: partial and complete.

Whether a violation was slight or major will be judged by the court. This helps the court assess what type of damages the party that breached the agreement ought to pay. The various terms and conditions that are required in a contract for the sale or purchase of real estate are stated in a real estate contract. A written or oral agreement is judged to have been violated if one of the parties does not carry out their half of the deal, as per the legislation regulating real estate transactions.

Navigating Changing Legal Regulations in Real Estate

Market News Real Estate Investments

For both industry professionals and homeowners alike, being abreast of new rules is vital in the ever-evolving world of real estate. Because these guidelines are continually changing, it's vital to respond to these changes as quickly as feasible. We'll speak about how to remain current with the real estate sector in this section, along with some practical ideas for managing the ever-changing legislation.

The Way Legal Regulations Work

Even within the same country, real estate laws and regulations could change substantially from one region to the next. These regulations are aimed to preserve the rights of buyers and sellers and to assure that real estate transactions are done ethically and in an orderly way. The dynamics of real estate laws are touched by numerous aspects, such as changes in governmental regulations, the position of the economy, and public preferences. Zoning regulations and land use limitations, for instance, may be revised to reflect changes in the patterns of urban expansion, and property tax laws may be amended to satisfy the needs of income.

Difficulties Real Estate Professionals Face

Professionals in the real estate market, such as developers, investors, property managers, and real estate brokers, are expected to stay up with any alterations to the legislation. Neglecting to take action may result in costly blunders, legal troubles, or missed prospects. These are a few of the issues they commonly encounter:

Observance

Real estate agents must prove they are in total compliance with local, state, and federal requirements. This requires being aware of tax requirements, building laws, zoning constraints, and fair housing legislation. Non-compliance may lead to fines, lawsuits, or even the inability to complete a transaction.

Volatility of the Market

Real estate rules are prone to swift changes in response to outside circumstances like the position of the economy. Real estate agents must promptly respond to these trends to secure their cash and make informed decisions.

Hazard Assessment

The real estate business is not without dangers. Liability, insurance demands, and property management strategies are all influenced by legal restrictions. Effective risk management is vital for professionals to preserve their assets and reputation.

Complexity of Transactions

Several legal paperwork, contracts, and negotiations are involved in real estate transactions. To minimize conflicts and ensure a flawless closing procedure, it is necessary to know the legal repercussions of each step.

Techniques for Handling Changing Legal Requirements

Real estate legal standards are continuously changing, so managing them entails being proactive and aware. The following strategies may aid industry specialists in staying ahead of these changes:

Ongoing Education

Continuing education and training should be a key focus for real estate professionals. This means attending lectures, workshops, and seminars that cover the legal elements of the field. Your long-term success hinges on keeping up with regulatory advancements.

Legal Advice

Building a connection with an experienced real estate lawyer may be highly useful. Attorneys may offer guidance on challenging legal situations, assess contracts, and guarantee compliance with all applicable laws.

Market Analysis

Regularly monitoring market trends and legislative developments is crucial. Gaining awareness about current and anticipated regulatory changes may be aided by networking with peers, joining professional organizations, and subscribing to industry journals.

Technological Instruments

Using technology to its maximum extent helps ease compliance activities. Software and digital platforms are tools that real estate brokers may use to track regulatory changes, execute contracts, and maintain precise record-keeping.

Cooperation

You may better handle intricate legal problems by collaborating with other professionals in the sector, such as mortgage brokers, appraisers, and property inspectors. Making better informed decisions could arise from sharing knowledge and experiences.

Flexibility

Professionals in the real estate sector need to be adaptable and ready to adjust course when requirements arise. This could involve changing modifications to investment plans, pricing, or marketing methods to meet new regulatory demands.

Capital

Financing your next venture with a real estate lender that can provide you the lowest rates and leverages is the easiest method to save money.

www.ingramcontent.com/pod-product-compliance
Lightning Source LLC
Chambersburg PA
CBHW071916210526
45479CB00002B/440